The Planets

Your Mission to Neptune

by Sally Kephart Carlson
illustrated by Scott Burroughs

Content Consultant
Diane M. Bollen, Research Scientist,
Cornell University

magic
Wagon

visit us at www.abdopublishing.com

Printed in the United States of America, North Mankato, Minnesota.
052011
092011

 THIS BOOK CONTAINS AT LEAST 10% RECYCLED MATERIALS.

Text by Sally Kephart Carlson
Illustrations by Scott Burroughs
Edited by Holly Saari
Series design and cover production by Becky Daum
Interior production by Christa Schneider

Library of Congress Cataloging-in-Publication Data
Carlson, Sally Kephart, 1970-
  Your mission to Neptune / by Sally Kephart Carlson ; illustrated by Scott Burroughs.
      p. cm. — (The planets)
  Includes index.
  ISBN 978-1-61641-681-2
  1. Neptune (Planet)—Juvenile literature. I. Burroughs, Scott, ill. II. Title.
QB691.C36 2012
  523.48—dc22
                          2011006777

Table of Contents

Imagine You Could Go

Where is Neptune in the night sky? Grab your binoculars. It's the only planet you can't see with just your eyes. At 2.7 billion miles (4.3 billion km) away from Earth, it's just too far!

You can't travel there, either. But imagine if you could . . .

Neptune's Appearance

All aboard! You're leaving Earth on a mission to the eighth and last planet in our solar system. Luckily, you have the fastest rocket ever made. You'll be there in no time.

After you pass Uranus, your next stop is Neptune. Have your camera ready. Neptune is brilliantly blue. Have you ever seen the blue flame on a stove? The gas being burned is methane. It's the same gas making Neptune's atmosphere look blue.

Size and Days

This blue planet is huge. About 60 Earths could fit inside of it! A fast jet would take two days to fly all the way around Earth. The same jet would take eight days to fly all the way around Neptune!

Even though Neptune is four times bigger than Earth, it spins a little faster. One rotation equals one day. Earth takes 24 hours to spin once. Neptune's day is only 16 hours.

Ball of Gases

Forget about landing on Neptune. There is no solid ground. Instead, Neptune has violently swirling clouds of gases.

These gases make up Neptune's atmosphere. The atmosphere is mostly lightweight hydrogen, some helium, and a sprinkling of methane ice.

Temperature

Be prepared as you dip into the clouds. Neptune's upper atmosphere is –330 degrees Fahrenheit (–201°C). It is the coldest planet in our solar system. If you didn't have a special space suit on, you would freeze in an instant!

The Windy Place

If that wasn't enough, you'll also have to battle Neptune's winds. Neptune is the windiest planet in the solar system. Winds can blow more than 1,500 miles per hour (2,414 km/h). On Earth, that's about the speed of 12 tornadoes rolled into one.

The winds can blow in huge storms that are the size of Earth. They look like dark spots from far away.

Energy Source

Where is the energy coming from to make such strong winds? You remember reading that wind is caused by areas of high pressure and low pressure. These differences in pressure are caused by the sun's energy.

But Neptune is too far from the sun for it to stir up the planet's atmosphere. Does Neptune have a hidden source of heat inside it? You'll have to find out!

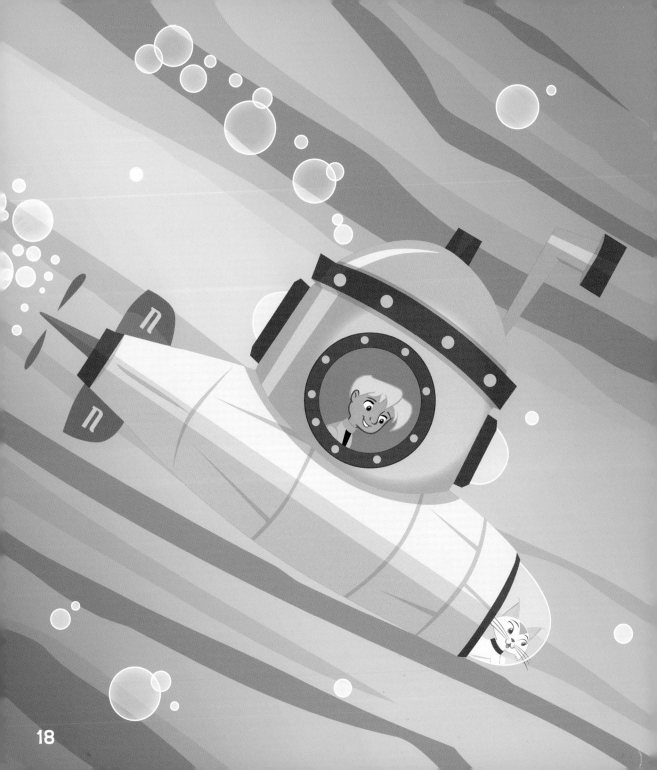

Liquid Layer

You're curious to find out what is below Neptune's atmosphere. You travel farther into the planet. You're about to reach the huge mantle of Neptune. This is the layer that comes after a planet's crust.

What is that ahead? It's liquid! Before you explore further, you convert your rocket into a submarine. The temperature and atmospheric pressure slowly increase. The ices in the atmosphere gradually melt into superheated liquids.

Parts of the mantle reach 5,000 degrees Fahrenheit (2,760°C)!

The atmospheric pressure is so great in the mantle that no heat can escape as vapor. Water, methane, and ammonia are forced to stay liquid. They can only become hotter and hotter.

You dive through the hot liquid and reach Neptune's core. It is as big as Earth. You're really starting to get warm in your suit. The molten metals here are as hot as the surface of the sun!

Years

You've been so busy, you forgot it's your birthday! Thankfully you haven't celebrated all your birthdays on Neptune. You would have been 165 Earth-years old on your first birthday here.

Why is this? Each planet orbits the sun. That is one year. Earth takes 365 days to orbit the sun. Neptune takes 60,190 days!

In 2011, Neptune completed its first orbit since it was discovered in 1846.

Seasons

Both Earth and Neptune are tilted as they orbit. So, different areas of the planet take turns facing the sun. That is how seasons change.

Back up on the surface, you travel to the south pole. It's summertime there. Neptune's long orbit makes for long seasons. It has been summertime at the south pole for 40 years! But don't get out your sandals. It's only warmed up to −310 degrees Fahrenheit (−190°C).

The Rings

Now you must escape Neptune's super strong gravity that's pulling you toward the planet. Crank up your jet pack, and power over to check out Neptune's six rings.

From Earth it looks like there are chunks missing from the rings. But up close, you have a better view. Some parts of the rings have more rock particles. This makes those parts of the ring look thicker from far away.

Moons

You have some time to visit Triton. It is the biggest of Neptune's 13 moons. It is also the coldest place in the solar system. You zoom around to Neptune's other moons. They are much smaller. Some are only 20 miles (32 km) across.

In the future, more amazing facts will be known about big, blue Neptune. Some discoveries will be made from Earth. Some will be made through space missions. Maybe an important discovery about Neptune will be made by you!

How Do Scientists Know about Neptune?

In the 1600s, Galileo Galilei first used a telescope. He was the first person to see Neptune, but he thought it was a star.

In the 1700s, brilliant scientist Isaac Newton wondered: What keeps the planets in their orbits? He wondered if the gravity on Earth was the same force that arranged the motion of planets and moons in space. He invented a type of math, calculus, that could determine the size and change of gravitational forces.

Scientists noticed Uranus had a little wobble in its orbit. They wondered if something nearby had a gravitational force pulling on Uranus. Using Newton's calculus, they proved it was possible that there could be a planet there. In 1846, scientists confirmed Neptune was there.

In 1989, *Voyager 2* flew near Neptune. It is the first and only spacecraft to have done so. Its cameras, telescopes, and computer technology collected pictures and most of the information known about Neptune.

NASA's *New Horizon* spacecraft is scheduled to cross Neptune's orbit on August 24, 2014. Scientists are excited to see what it will discover!

Neptune Facts

Position: Eighth planet from the sun and last in our solar system

Distance from sun: 2.8 billion miles (4.5 billion km)

Diameter (distance through the planet's middle): 30,775 miles (49,528 km)

Length of orbit (year): 165 Earth years

Length of rotation (day): About 16 hours

Gravity: 14 percent stronger than Earth's gravity

Number of moons: At least 13

Atmosphere temperature: −330 degrees Fahrenheit (−201°C)

Words to Know

atmosphere—the layer of gases surrounding a planet.

core—the center of a planet.

gas—a substance that spreads out to fit what it is in, like air in a tire.

gravity—the force that pulls a smaller object toward a larger object.

mantle—the part of a planet between the crust and the core.

methane—odorless, colorless, flammable gas that reflects blue light.

orbit—to travel around something, usually in an oval path.

solar system—a star and the objects, such as planets, that travel around it.

Learn More

Books

Chrismer, Melanie. *Neptune*. New York: Children's Press, 2005.

Landau, Elaine. *Neptune*. New York: Children's Press, 2005.

Sherman, Josepha. *Neptune!* New York: Marshall Cavendish, 2010.

Trammel, Howard K. *The Solar System*. New York: Children's Press, 2010.

Web Sites

To learn more about Neptune, visit ABDO Group online at **www.abdopublishing.com**. Web sites about Neptune are featured on our Book Links page. These links are routinely monitored and updated to provide the most current information available.

Index